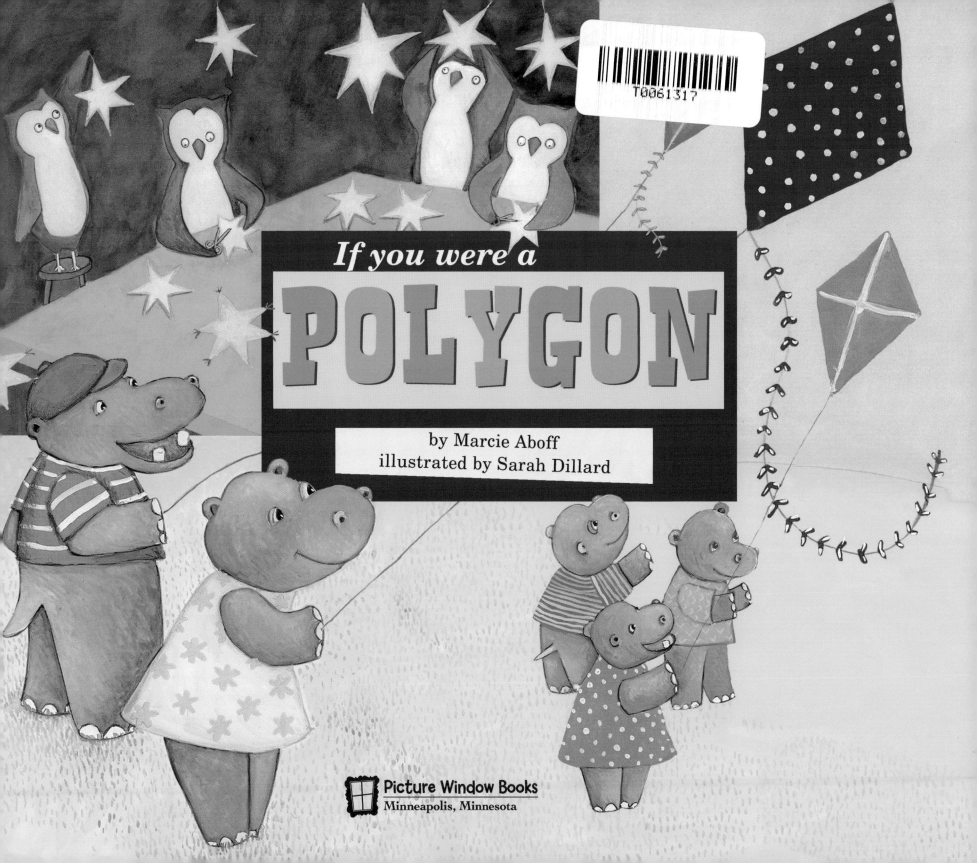

If you were a
POLYGON

by Marcie Aboff

illustrated by Sarah Dillard

Picture Window Books
Minneapolis, Minnesota

Editor: Jill Kalz
Designer: Lori Bye
Page Production: Melissa Kes
Art Director: Nathan Gassman
Editorial Director: Nick Healy
Creative Director: Joe Ewest
The illustrations in this book were created with
watercolor and gouache.

Picture Window Books
1710 Roe Crest Drive
North Mankato, MN 56003
www.capstonepub.com

Library of Congress Cataloging-in-Publication Data
Aboff, Marcie.
If you were a polygon / by Marcie Aboff ;
illustrated by Sarah Dillard.
p. cm. — (Math fun)
Includes index.
ISBN 978-1-4048-5512-0 (library binding)
ISBN 978-1-4048-5692-9 (paperback)
1. Polygons—Juvenile literature. 2. Shapes—Juvenile
literature. I. Dillard, Sarah, 1961- ill. II. Title.
QA482.A25 2010
516'.154—dc22   2009006889

Special thanks to our adviser for his expertise:

Stuart Farm, M.Ed., Mathematics Lecturer
University of North Dakota

Printed in the United States   5829

polygon—a flat, closed figure with three or more straight sides

If you were a polygon ...

... you could be found on the street,

up in the sky,

or on a house.

REX

If you were a polygon, you would be a flat, closed figure with three or more sides. All your sides would be straight.

NON-POLYGON TABLES

Pete and Patty shop for a new kitchen table. Some tables are polygons. Some are not.

The pink polygon table is perfect!

If you were a polygon, you could be a regular polygon. All your sides would be the same length. All your angles would be the same measure, too.

Piper obeys each regular polygon she sees.

STOP

She stops at a stop sign.

YIELD

She waits at a yield sign.

And she slows down at the crossing sign
to let her friends pass safely.

If you were a polygon, you could be an irregular polygon.
All your sides would not be the same length or your angles
would not be the same measure.

Howard, Hillary, and their three little hippos
fly kites in the park.

Each kite is an irregular polygon.

If you were a polygon, the points at which your sides meet would be called vertices. One point is called a vertex.

Ozzie and his friends cut paper stars and hang them.

Each star has 12 points, or vertices.

13

If you were a polygon, you could be a triangle.
You would have three sides.

Doogle draws his dream home.
The roof is shaped like a triangle.

Doogle

If you were a polygon, you could be a square or a rectangle. You would have four sides.

Doogle draws square windows.

The door is shaped like a rectangle.

Doogle

15

If you were a polygon, you could be a pentagon. You would have five sides.

The forest animals welcome their new bird neighbors.

Five squirrels hold a sign shaped like a pentagon.

If you were a polygon, you could be a hexagon, with six sides.
Or you could be a heptagon, with seven sides.

Six rabbits hold a sign
shaped like a hexagon.

Welcome!

Glad You're HERE!

Seven mice hold a heptagon-shaped sign.

If you were a polygon, you could be an octagon. You would have eight sides.

Ollie the octopus sleeps in a bed shaped like an octagon.

If you were a polygon, you could be a nonagon. You would have nine sides.

Carly and her eight sisters sleep in a nonagon-shaped bed.

Each cat gets one side of the bed.

If you were a polygon, you could be a decagon. You would have 10 sides.

Beautiful paintings hang in the Decagon Museum.
Each painting has 10 sides.

You would have at least three straight sides ...

STOP

... if you were a polygon.

SPOT THE POLYGONS

Look at the shapes below. How many are polygons? Of the shapes that are polygons, how many are regular polygons? How many are irregular polygons?

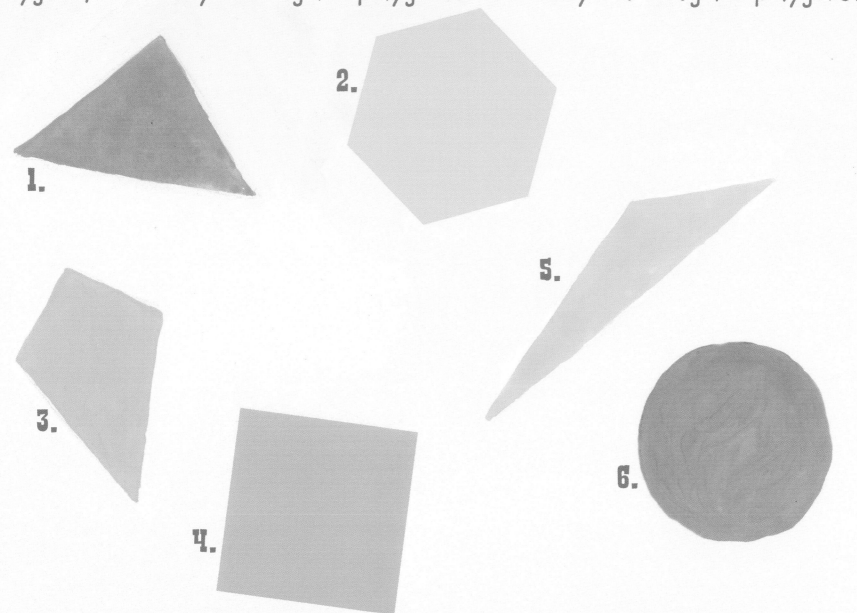

Glossary

angle—the measurement between two sides at a corner

decagon—a polygon with 10 sides

heptagon—a polygon with seven sides

hexagon—a polygon with six sides

irregular polygon—a polygon with sides that are not all the same length or angles that are not all the same measure

nonagon—a polygon with nine sides

octagon—a polygon with eight sides

polygon—a flat, closed figure with three or more straight sides

rectangle—an irregular polygon with four right angles

regular polygon—a polygon with sides that are all the same length and angles that are all the same measure

square—a regular polygon with four sides

triangle—a polygon with three sides

vertex/vertices—the point(s) where two sides meet

To Learn More

More Books to Read

Ferrell, Karen. *The Great Polygon Caper.* Hauppauge, N.Y.: Barrons Educational Series, 2008.

Leech, Bonnie Coulter. *Polygons.* New York: Powerkids Press, 2007.

Internet Sites

FactHound offers a safe, fun way to find Internet sites related to this book. All of the sites on FactHound have been researched by our staff.

Here's all you do:

Visit www.facthound.com

FactHound will fetch the best sites for you!

Look for all of the books in the Math Fun series:

If You Were a Circle

If You Were a Divided-by Sign

If You Were a Fraction

If You Were a Minus Sign

If You Were a Minute

If You Were a Plus Sign

If You Were a Polygon

If You Were a Pound or a Kilogram

If You Were a Quadrilateral

If You Were a Quart or a Liter

If You Were a Set

If You Were a Times Sign

If You Were a Triangle

If You Were an Even Number

If You Were an Inch or a Centimeter

If You Were an Odd Number